THE Family Rescue ™ KIT&GUIDE

AIRPORT EDITION

VolumeOne

by Suzi Berg

www.FamilyRescueKits.com

THE Family Rescue™ KIT&GUIDE AIRPORT EDITION

Copyright © 2010 by Suzi Berg. All rights reserved.

suzjqz.productions Publishing Group
Laguna Niguel, CA 92677 • 949-388-5486
www.FamilyRescueKits.com

ISBN -978-0-983034-1-7 • LCCN - 2010937727

Book sales for North America and International:
suzjqz.productions, Laguna Niguel, CA 92677
Toll free: 1.888.9.KIDKIT (954-3548)
Email: orders@FamilyRescueKits.com

Printed in both the United States of America and China

www.FamilyRescueKits.com

TABLE OF CONTENTS

CHAPTERS

Recommended items to add to your Activity Kit

1. A bottle of approved travel-size hand sanitizer.

2. M&Ms, licorice, jelly beans, trail mix or other small, colorful treats for immediate rewards and point counters. ***Recommended: Licorice (good for the digestion) and small treats sweetened with fruit juice.*** Also, be sure to load up with healthy snacks like dried fruit, granola bars, crackers, cheese, etc.

3. A small, portable DVD player, *LeapFrog* or *iPod* loaded with games, two or more movies, and a headset.

To order additional books, *activity kits* or *refill kits* visit:

www.FamilyRescueKits.com

"We don't stop playing because we grow old.
We grow old because we stop playing."
– George B. Shaw

DEDICATION

This book is dedicated to my darling daughter, Kira who
is my inspiration & the love of my life. Also, to all the
parents & caretakers who see the value in connecting with
their children through love & laughter, every day, thereby
turning travel troubles into fun family experiences.

ACKNOWLEDGEMENTS

While checking into our flight to Hawaii for a much overdue vacation, I noticed a little boy, about two or three years old, about to walk out of the airport door into the sea of taxis and cars buzzing about! With a then three-year-old of my own, I quickly alerted the mom who frantically instructed her older son to go and retrieve his brother.

It was this incident that inspired the *Treasure Hunt* game and also the need for this book.

It is with great pleasure I present *The Family Rescue Kit & Guide™ — Airport Edition*, in the same spirit as ***The Restaurant Rescue Kit & Guide™***. This is for all of you who have had similar struggles. I am confident it will make travel more fun with less hassles and turn potential nightmares into dream vacations come true!

Introduction

The Trick is to Find The Fun

If you have traveled with children, you know the struggles. Getting packed and to the airport in time is enough of a challenge. But once you get there, how do you manage the luggage, check in, make it through security in time–all without your children running out the airport door or having a complete melt-down?

If you've successfully made it to the gate early or if your flight is delayed, what do you do while you wait to prepare your kids for the long, cramped plane ride? And last but not least, what about that long, cramped plane ride?!

Rest easy! The games in this book will not only help make your trip FUN, but will also educate and entertain your children, all while you get to know them on a whole new level.

Based on the old principle, "When there is a task that must be done, the trick is to find the fun!" from the movie, *Mary Poppins*, this book will help you *enjoy* your travel time with your kids using fun, simple methods while also incorporating safety. This book will help you turn a potentially dangerous and always stressful trip into a safe, fun family adventure!

Prepare for a Great Trip!

You will be best served by this book by reading it through ahead of time and playing some of the games before you leave on your trip. This will familiarize you with your new "arsenal of fun" and help you determine which games your children enjoy the most. That way, should you find yourself in need of a "rescue," you will know what to do.

Be creative! As you work through the games, add extra items to your kit that your children are especially fond of, and include action figures, dolls or favorite small toys they find comforting.

Travel Tips for Tots

- Fill out and attach one *Airport Rescue Information Tag* (provided in the back of this book) for each child before you leave for the airport! Place it inside their clothing where it can be found if needed, but is not visible to strangers.

- Before take off or landing, take two Styrofoam cups and fill them with hot water, then empty. Place the cups immediately over your child's ears. The cooling may relieve the pressure fluctuations that often cause pain in the ears. Another way to relieve ear pressure is to have them chew gum, eat a snack or drink water during take off and landing.

- Keep a small bottle of hand sanitizer in your zip lock bag for approved travel fluids and use it on your children's hands often.

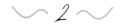

Chapter 1

PREPARING to Leave

Use the following games to get your kids to help you prepare for your trip *and still have fun!* These games include creative ways for children to pack their own bags, and can even serve to help you remember the things that need to be done before your departure.

"Pick-Pack-Go"

Make a game out of packing! Tell your child that her dresser, closet, etc. has magically turned into a "vacation travel store." Lay out your child's suitcase and tell her this is her "Vacation Treasure Chest." On a piece of paper, make a tick-tack-toe grid. In each square, draw a simple picture of what you would like her to pack and label it (e.g. sock, shoe, shirt, etc.) On the back, indicate how many of these items she needs to bring. *Tip: Make copies of this for future trips.*

Tear the paper in sections so that there is one labeled picture on each square. Mix them up and fan them out, turn them face-side down or just let her throw them all in the air and try to catch one. Next, have her find and pack the items on that square and give the paper back to you when she has done so. Continue doing this until you have all the squares back and she is all packed!

"Playing It Safe"

K nowledge is power! Empower your children with vital information that can save you some time, or in an emergency, perhaps even save their lives.

Inside the Airport

- What do we do before we sit on any airport toilet seat? *Answer: Wipe with soap and water or hand sanitizer.*

- Where are you going? *Answer: Your destination city and state and hotel name or person's name you are visiting.*

- On what airline are you flying? What are your flight and gate numbers?

- What should you do if you get lost? *Answer: STAY IN THE AREA. Go directly to the nearest gate and ask the people behind the counter to page your parents.*

- What should you do if a stranger tries to take your hand? *Answer: Scream and run!*

- What is your caretaker's mobile phone number?

- Where is the exit that is nearest your seat?

- How do you use an *Air Phone* or mobile phone and who would you call? Go over the instructions listed on the air phone with your child and decide who they should call in an emergency. Practice making a call on a mobile phone and go over what they should say.

"Treasure Hunt"

Kids of all ages love presents! Anything they have not seen before (or for along time!) is always a sure hit. This game will keep your kids glued to your luggage until it's checked in instead of worrying about them running about while you are distracted by the check-in process.

Before you leave, take a trip to your local *Dollar* or *99¢ Store.* Pick out several small, age-appropriate toys for each child, such as toy planes, books (story, coloring game) puzzles, *Mad Libs,* magnet toys, action figures, etc. Be sure to include a special treasure bag for them to gather the toys in. You can do this secretly or with your children.

Distribute the toys into easily accessible outside pockets of the luggage. On the day of your trip, give each child a "Treasure Bag." Once you reach the airport, gauge the time you feel you have before check-in based on how long the line is.

The object of the game is to find as many of the toys as possible before your luggage is checked in. Let your children take turns. They ALL *must stay near the luggage* and hunt for the toys in order to keep them. There will be no misbehaving or running around so they can find and keep their new toys, and they now have new treasures to help keep them busy the rest of the trip. The toys can be easily stored in the treasure bag and placed inside their carry-on luggage when not in use.

Chapter 2

Navigating the Airport

Use the following games to help get your children through security and to the gate safely. Remember, practicing the games before you leave will make them more effective after your trip is underway.

"Every Squeeze Counts"

Keep your child wanting to hold your hand using this simple game and reward with treats or points. This game works with one or two parents holding the child's hands. Squeeze her hand a certain number of times. Then ask her to tell you how many times her hands were squeezed. For a bigger challenge, if there are two of you, ask her to add the two numbers and tell you the total. Correct answers receive points.

"Monster Hand"

If trying to hold your child's hand is a problem, try this! Make believe your hand is a "Monster" or "Gator" hand and have it snapping open and shut at your side. Your child will be trying to put his hand in yours without the "monster" getting him, staying by your side, giggling all the way to the gate!

"Eye-Spy"

An old classic! Call out an object usually found in an airport and say, "I spy a family." or "I spy a bathroom." Have your child count as many of those objects as she can along the way. Be sure to have her spot your gate number and letter, and tell YOU where to go next!

Another way to play is to go through the alphabet and take turns finding something that starts with each letter. Turn the game into *Follow the Leader* with you following her lead as she finds the gate or vice-versa.

"I Can, Can You?"

Take turns challenging your kids to do something that you can do, and/or that you want them to learn how to do. The Challenger does it first and then everyone else has to try (e.g. pat your head and rub your tummy at the same time). Take advantage of this game to teach safety and travel tips. *(For a list of suggestions, see Appendix A.)*

"The Security Line Dance"

Get ready for some fun in the security line! This game will not only help you get through the line faster, but will have your child performing the security requirements as though they were fun games.

While in the security line, tell your children they are going to do the *Security Line Dance*. Instruct them that to perform this dance, they must first take off their shoes and put them in the "Magic Tunnel" (aka the x-ray machine), so they can receive their "Dancing Dust." Have them place their shoes in the "magic" rolling trays that lead to the tunnel.

The children must then perform the dance steps as they go through the "Magic Gate" (aka the metal detector) to transfer the steps to the shoes as they go through the tunnel! If she is a little ballerina, let her twirl through and put her arms up. If you have a little boy, tell him to do the *Monster* or *Robot* dance with his arms out, taking big steps.

Once your belongings are through, bring them to the area provided for re-packing and tell your children to find their shoes, put them back on and test them to see if they can do the same twirls and steps your children did with them off. This gives you time to gather the rest of your things.

Let your children twirl, dance and monster-step all the way to the gate!

Chapter 3

Gate Games

Use the following games once you've made it to the gate. They will be very helpful if your flight is delayed or if you have somehow managed to make it this far a little early!

"The Big Draw Back"

Have your child either sit on your lap or turn her back to you. Tell her you are going to "draw" a letter or number on her back with your finger. Be very slow and deliberate. Repeat as necessary. Have her guess what you drew! To make it a bit more challenging, also draw simple pictures such as a cat or smiley face.

"Flight Attendant"

If this is not your child's first time on a plane, have him pretend to be the flight attendant. Pretend you are on the plane and let him tell you how to buckle your seat belt, what to do if the cabin loses pressure, where your exits and bathrooms are and that your seat cushion is a flotation device. Have him use all the hand motions. Once your child has played this game, he will surely pay closer attention to the attendant so he can do an even better job the next time he plays it.

"State That State"

Have your child name the states in the U.S. starting with the one you are traveling to, then tell some facts about it (e.g. its capitol, nickname etc.). Use the map on the next page to show your child your trip.

State	Capitol	Abbrev	Fact	State	Capitol	Abbrev	Fact
• Alabama	Montgomery	AL	Yellow Hammer	• Montana	Helena	MT	Dinosaur Park
• Alaska	Juneau	AK	Snow & Cold	• Nebraska	Lincoln	NE	Corn
• Arkansas	Little Rock	AR	Ozark Mts.	• Nevada	Carson City	NV	Las Vegas
• Arizona	Phoenix	AZ	Grand Canyon	• N Hampshire	Concord	NH	Granite
• California	Sacramento	CA	Golden Gate	• New Jersey	Trenton	NJ	Garden State
• Colorado	Denver	CO	Centennial	• New Mexico	Santa Fe	NM	Enchantment
• Connecticut	Hartford	CT	Constitution	• New York	Albany	NY	Statue of Liberty
• Delaware	Dover	DE	First State	• N Carolina	Raleigh	NC	Tar Heels
• Florida	Tallahassee	FL	Gators/Orange	• N Dakota	Bismarck	ND	Rough Rider
• Georgia	Atlanta	GA	Peaches	• Ohio	Columbus	OH	Buckeye
• Hawaii	Honolulu	HI	Rainbows	• Oklahoma	Oklahoma City	OK	Sooner
• Idaho	Boise	ID	Gem & Potato	• Oregon	Salem	OR	Beaver
• Illinois	Springfield	IL	Lincoln Fort	• Pennsylvania	Harrisburg	PA	Pretzels
• Indiana	Indianapolis	IN	Hoosiers	• Rhode Island	Providence	RI	Ocean State
• Iowa	Des Moines	IA	Hawkeye State	• S Carolina	Columbia	SC	Palmetto
• Kansas	Topeka	KS	Sunflower	• S Dakota	Pierre	SD	Mt. Rushmore
• Kentucky	Frankfort	KY	Horse Racing	• Tennessee	Nashville	TN	Volunteer
• Louisiana	Baton Rouge	LA	Pelicans	• Texas	Austin	TX	Lone Star
• Maine	Augusta	ME	Pines & Moose	• Utah	Salt Lake City	UT	Beehive
• Maryland	Annapolis	MD	Free	• Vermont	Montpelier	VT	Skiing
• Massachusetts	Boston	MA	Bay State	• Virginia	Richmond	VA	Old Dominion
• Michigan	Lansing	MI	Wolverine	• Washington	Olympia	WA	Apples & Rain
• Minnesota	St. Paul	MN	10,000 Lakes	• West Virginia	Charleston	WV	Mountains
• Mississippi	Jackson	MS	Magnolia	• Wisconsin	Madison	WI	Badger
• Missouri	Jefferson City	MO	Gateway Arch	• Wyoming	Cheyenne	WY	Old Faithful

The United States of America

"Color Me Mine"

Ask your child how many things of a certain color he can find within view. Have him keep count. If it's just the two of you, take turns and let him pick the next color. You find the objects or find them together.

A variation of this game is to call out a color and take turns naming every object of that color that you can think of (i.e. **RED** would be "Exit Sign," "clown nose," "Jell-O," etc.).

"I Packed A Bag..."

Players begin by saying, "I went to London (or Hawaii or Grandma's) and in my bag I packed..." Each person takes a turn and must tell what was packed and why. The next person states what was packed already, adds his or her own item and tells why. Outrageous items are even more fun!

"Sounds of Silence"

Everyone is silent for about fifteen seconds and must listen to what is going on around them. Take turns listing all the things you all heard (e.g. flight announcements, people talking, cash registers ringing, planes landing, etc.).

"The Memory Game"

Player is told to take a good look around him (this game can also be played on the plane) and notice as many details as he can. He should then close his eyes. Then ask him to remember what he saw! Make the questions age-appropriate. *Tip: Use a napkin or item of clothing as a blindfold to make it easier for him not to look.* Here are some suggestions to get started:

- Is the flight or gate attendant a man or a woman?

- How many flight / gate attendants are there?

- What are you wearing? What is he (your child) wearing?

- Where is the nearest bathroom? (if on the plane, exit?)

- Is the person seated to the right (or left) of you a man, woman or child?

- What is your flight and gate number?

- How many bags are we taking on the plane?

- How many planes are within view?

- What color is the seat, tray, carpet, etc.?

- Was anyone sitting nearby eating / sleeping / on the phone?

- What is the name of the store that is closest to your gate?

"Oldies But Goodies"

While waiting at the gate, we have had a lot of laughs playing very old and simple games, such as *Simon Says*, *Red Light, Green Light*, *May I?* and *Freeze Dance*.

Keep track of points to make it more fun! With *Simon Says* and *May I?* the object is to only do the things that begin with "Simon says..." or after the child asks, *May I?* In *Red Light, Green Light*, they can only take steps on green, must slow down on yellow and stop on red. In *Freeze Dance*, sing a song or use your phone or iPod, and suddenly be silent. They can dance as long as there is music or singing but must freeze during the silence.

"Gate Dance"

Using some of the string from your *Activity Kit*, make a circle in an open space near where you are waiting for your plane. Play the *Hokey-Pokey!* Put in your right foot, then left foot; head, bottom, right and left hands, etc. and shake them all around. Do the *Hokey-Pokey* and turn yourself around. That's what it's all about! You can also do the *Bunny Hop* together if there is enough space.

Chapter 4

on the plane

The following games are designed for play in close quarters, such as once you are seated on the plane. Use them when your child feels the need to interact and connect with you. Be aware of which games are appropriate considering the passengers around you (e.g. if someone is sleeping next to you, choose a quieter game). *Tip: A small portable DVD player or iPod with headphones, loaded with games and movies, is invaluable on long flights to give yourself a break and time to rest.*

"Edible Art"

Here is a great way to make FUN out of those boring pretzel and snack packs. Use the pretzels, cheese doodles and other snacks to create all

kinds of funny pictures before you eat them! You will be amazed at what you and your children will come up with.

Tip: Bring your own food or purchase something healthy at the airport to eat on the plane.

"Every Passenger Counts"

This game is wonderful for developing observation skills and will help children become aware of their surroundings; skills that could one day save their lives.

When the seat belt sign is off, every once in awhile, declare an "Observation Round" and take your child on a stroll up and down the plane. Ask him to count how many people are _____ (pick one or two from the list below.) This is especially helpful after viewing a movie or taking a nap. Instruct him to count silently and give the number when you sit back down so you don't disturb other passengers.

- Wearing scarfs, sweaters or other type of clothing.
- Sleeping, eating chewing gum, reading, using a computer.
- Wearing red (or a favorite color).
- Are men, women, babies or children.
- Have blonde / red / brunette hair.
- Are waiting for the bathroom.
- Have their shoes off.
- Look happy / bored / sad.
- Talking to a traveling companion.
- Said "hello" or smiled as you walked by.

"What Am I?"

Think of a person, place or animal, and announce your chosen category, along with two clues (I am an animal that says "Oink" and lives on a farm.). Player must guess what you are by asking questions. *(For a list of suggestions, see Appendix B.)*

Another way to play this is to have your child draw an object from the category on the Doodle Pad and turn it over. Everyone takes turns guessing what it is before he proudly reveals it.

"True or False?"

Player listens to a statement and then has to determine whether or not it is true or false. Try to use travel related statements and begin each sentence with, "True or False."

- The person in front of you **LOVES IT** when you kick the seat. **(False.)**

- As soon as the seat belt sign is off, you should jump up and run up and down the plane aisles. **(False.)**

- When the plane is taking off or landing, you should be in your seat belt. **(True.)**

- The floor lights up and shows you where the exit doors are if there is an emergency landing. **(True.)**

- The plane has to go at least 200 mph in order to take off. **(True.)**

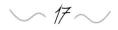

"Read My Lips"

A plane engine can be very loud, making it difficult to hear each other during your flight. Try doing charades, mouthing simple words or phrases while also using hand symbols and have your children guess what you are saying!

"Very Handy"

Remember these two classics? All you need are your hands, so you can play anywhere! Try to trap each other's thumb in *Thumb Wars*, or play good ol' *Rock, Paper Scissors!* Rock: a closed fist. Paper: an open palm. Scissors: two fingers in a sideways "V" shape. A rock wins by crushing scissors; scissors win by cutting paper and paper wins by covering a rock.

"The Words of the Day Are..."

This game is great for developing word skills! Simply spell out today's date (e.g. J-A-N-U-A-R-Y S-E-V-E-N-T-H) and challenge your children to spell as many words as they can, using only the letters in today's date. Some of the "hidden" words in this date are: sent, save, ran, run, ten, vent, have, tree, hear, say, true, net, yes, never, try, near, tear, hat, even and year. Can you find any more?

"Silly Alphabet One-Liners!"

Start with A and go through the alphabet. Take turns making a funny statement using only words starting with that letter or letter sound. Filler words are allowed and the sentences don't have to make sense:

- Amy Ant ambled around after she ate all the apples.
- Ben the bear began begging for bananas beneath a big, brown bench.
- Captain Calvin, the creepy cowboy, says candy corn can create cavities.
- Fran fed Fred fancy fried falafels but they made him feel fat.
- Gracey, the girl gorilla, giggled as she gobbled grapes and gumdrops.
- Monster monsoons made Michael's mom miss many months of mail.
- Nellie, there is no need for Ned to nag Nillie now.
- Perhaps Peter was too pooped to picked a peck of pickled peppers.
- Tiny Timmy tossed tomatoes turning the tacos into tornadoes.
- Uma the Ukranian unicorn utilized a U-turn with an ultrasonic umbrella.
- Alex was excited to x-ray the exit sign.
- Young Yolanda yelled and yodeled, yet ate yummy yellow yogurt in the yard.
- Zany zombie zebras with zits zoomed and zigzagged through the zoo.

"Mini Pictionary"

Take a piece of paper from the note pad included in your *Activity Kit* or another source, and tear it into ten pieces. Using things your child is familiar with, write down short phrases, movies, siblings names, objects, animals, etc., placing one on each piece of paper. Put the pieces in a cup. Player picks one piece of paper, looks at it, and has 30 seconds to draw something that makes you say what was on the paper without speaking!

"The Big Face-Off"

Take turns describing a situation that would make someone happy, sad, angry, afraid or surprised, etc. Everyone makes a face to express how they would feel. Vote on who made the best face. *(For a list of suggestions, see Appendix C.)*

"Animal Alphabet"

This game is great fun and also requires thinking skills. The first player names an animal that starts with the letter "A." Within ten seconds, the next player names an animal that starts with the letter "B," etc. Each player must name the next animal within the specified time or say "pass." Reward success with points or treats. There are many possible variations, such as animals that live in the water, have fur, fly, or other categories such as states, food, colors, people you know, etc.

"Travel Trivia"

Ask trivia questions about traveling and your destination. The questions can be about travel safety, facts about where you are going or who your are visiting, etc. Here are some suggestions:

- What is the capitol of your home state? Your destination?
- Is your destination near mountains or an ocean?
- What is the name of the ocean or mountain range you will be near?
- Will it be cold or hot where you are going?
- What is the name of the city and state you are visiting?
- Name one fact about the place you are visiting.
- What is the name of the hotel or place you will be staying?
- Will you be on an island? Which one?
- Name something fun you will do on this trip.
- Name a food you like to eat on vacation.
- Where is your favorite place to go for vacation?
- What country are you traveling to?
- What is your favorite thing about staying in a hotel?
- What do you like about flying in an airplane?

"Lines and Dots"

Make a grid (or have your child make one) of dots on a sheet of paper (see below.) Each player takes turns drawing a horizontal or vertical line between two dots that are next to each other. No diagonal lines allowed. When a player makes a complete square, he marks the square with his initials in the center of it, and then takes another turn. The player with the most initialed squares at the end wins!

"Ad Lip"

Wonderful for the imagination! Simply start a sentence and have your child fill in the blanks. Keep doing this until you have an entire story. Say something like, "I was walking down a _____ and I saw a big _____ ." or "We went on a treasure hunt at the park. The first treasure I found was a _____. So I put it in my _____. But then I came across a _____ ." Keep the story going based on how your child fills in the blanks.

"USA Landmark Matching Game"

Where are these great landmarks located? Match the description to the pictures. Take this opportunity to teach your child about these famous places. *(See answers below.)*

1

Niagara Falls, Niagara Falls, NY

Capitol Building, Washington, DC

Gateway Arch, St. Louis, MO

2

Mt. Rushmore, Keystone, SD

Golden Gate Bridge, San Francisco, CA

Liberty Bell, Philadelphia, PA

Statue of Liberty, New York City, NY

3

Lincoln Memorial, Washington, DC

Grand Canyon, Williams, AZ

Everglades, Everglades Park, FL

4

10

9

8

5 **6** **7**

Answers: 1. Statue of Liberty; 2. Capitol Building; 3. Golden Gate Bridge; 4. Liberty Bell; 5. Grand Canyon; 6. Mt. Rushmore; 7. Niagara Falls; 8. Gateway Arch; 9. Lincoln Memorial; 10. Everglades

"Memory Game"

The following games help develop memory and reasoning skills and can be played anywhere. My daughter requests one or more of these games almost every time we are out running an errand, at a restaurant, or somewhere that requires a bit of a wait.

Game 1: Count from one to ten or twenty, depending on your child's age. Leave out one number and ask her what number you skipped.

Game 2: Go through part of the alphabet or spell a simple word, skipping one of the letters. Your child gets to fill in the missing letter! This game can also be played on the *Doodle Pad.*

Game 3: Using the kings, queens, aces and jacks, turn the cards face down. Take turns finding matches! Whoever gets the most matches wins. For a longer game, add some pairs of numbers.

"The Find-Your-Card Mix-Up"

Pull one of each: ace, king, queen, jack from a deck of cards. Have your child pick any card he likes from the rest of the deck. Place his card along with the four other cards, all face-up so he can see where his card is. Then turn them all over.

Ask him to keep an eye on his card as you move them around, switching them with the other four cards on the table. Let him guess which one is his card, seeing how many guesses it takes to find it!

Chapter 5

Activity Kit Games

As you play these games, cup your hands over the dice as you roll so they stay on your tray table. Uncover them and look only after they have stopped moving.

"On A Roll"

Game 1: Ask your child to call out a number from one to ten. Then have him roll the dice into a bowl or cup his hands over them. If his number comes up, he wins. If his numbers are not rolled, he can still win bonus points by correctly adding the numbers that are showing on the dice.

Game 2: Roll one of the dice to determine the number to be played (e.g. six.) First player gets all five dice and rolls all of them at once, trying for sixes, setting all the sixes he gets aside. Count how many rolls it takes to get them all showing sixes. The second player does the same. Whoever gets all the dice showing sixes in the least amount of rolls wins!

Game 3: Using all five dice, each player has three tries to roll a poker hand, such as a full house (two of one number; three of another); three or four of a kind; a large straight (five consecutive numbers) or a small straight (four consecutive numbers). The highest valid poker hand wins! All five dice showing the same number wins **DOUBLE POINTS.**

"Letter Roll"

These games help develop spelling and reading skills. Take this opportunity to teach your children how to spell their names and other familiar words.

Game 1: Fill up a square with the alphabet dice, (or have your children do it!) being sure to spell a word or two within the square. Ask your children to find the hidden words, or find the ones they spelled!

Game 2: Ask your children to choose a word to spell and roll for the correct letters. Keep rolling until they spell the entire word.

Game 3: Roll all of the dice onto the tray table and ask your children to spell words using only the letters that are showing. Give points or treats for each word they create!

"You're on Candid Camera!"

This is a really great game to get to know how your child thinks! According to his ability to handle this equipment, either allow your child to use your digital camera, or buy one made for children his age. Encourage him to take pictures of whatever he finds interesting. Look at all the pictures on the preview and ask him to explain why he took each one.

"Guess the Object"

Place a few small objects in a paper bag or large cloth napkin or T-shirt. Use one of each of the objects included in your *Activity Kit*, and/or other small items from your purse or carry-on that are familiar to your child.

Let her see and feel the objects as they are being placed into the bag, then close it up. If you are using a napkin, T-shirt or other piece of clothing, allow holes in the sides as shown below.

Next, name or ask her to name one of the objects that you placed inside and then let her reach in and find that object without looking.

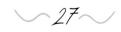

Squeals of delight will follow as she finds the right object!

As an alternative, you can have her close her eyes, place an object in her hand and ask her to guess what it is.

"Pipe-Dream Creations"

Have your children use the pipe cleaners and beads provided in the *Activity Kit* to make a variety of animals, shapes, objects, insects and people! While the girls create their **Kitchen Sink Jewelry**, the boys can make *Pipe-Dream Creations*. Use the creations as characters and make up stories. Watch your childrens' imaginations take over!

Create challenges for them by suggesting they make a spider or other familiar object. *(See the next two pages for instructions on how to create a flower and other creatures.)*

"Kitchen Sink Jewelry"

Use the pipe cleaners, paper clips, beads and clay included in your *Activity Kit* to make bracelets, anklets, headbands, ponytail holders, tiaras and necklaces. *(Tip: Pour the beads into a cup or bowl to help keep them off the floor.)* To keep the beads from sliding off the pipe cleaner, bend the end into a knot. Add things from home, such as colorful doughnut-shaped cereals and macaroni for even more fun. When your jewelry is finished, simply twist the ends together. *(See the examples provided on page 32.)*

"Pipe-Dream Creation Examples"

Snail

Start by coiling one of the pipe cleaners around your finger to make the head and attach it to one of the pipe cleaners as shown on right.

Attach two of the remaining pipe cleaners together. The example to the right shows two different colors to better help you see how to connect them.

Flower

Start with the pieces shown to the right. Make the stem and leaf as shown. Make a circle out of two yellow pipe cleaners, coiling them around. Attach the coil to the stem.

Use the remaining pipe cleaners to make the petals, bending or coiling them, and attaching them as shown.

Next, coil the two attached pipe cleaners around to make the shell and attach to the body and head.

Finally, add a pair of sticker eyes from your *Activity Kit* and give him (or her) a name!

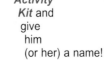

Green Fly

Take a green pipe cleaner and coil it by wrapping it around your finger.

Next, add two beads at the end and secure by tucking it into the body.

Use another color for the wings and bend as shown. Then wrap around the body.

Snake

Connect three pipe cleaners at the top and teach your child to braid them for the body. Coil another pipe cleaner around your finger to make the head and attach it to the body, letting the end stick out for the tongue.

Lastly, take a yellow pipe cleaner and wrap it around the braided body. Finish with the eye stickers and shape as desired.

Coiled Head

"Kitchen Sink Jewelry" Examples

Headbands, Bracelets & Necklaces

To make these pieces, start by curling up the end of a pipe cleaner to hold the beads in place. Add beads, paper clips, clay balls, round cereal and/or macaroni to design your jewelry.

When a longer piece is desired, simply twist two or more pipe cleaners together. Endless possibilities!

Make necklaces, headbands, ponytail holders, bracelets, anklets, belts, etc.

"Clay Play"

Use the non-toxic, multi-colored clay provided in your *Activity Kit* to make all kinds of amazing objects, animals, people, scenes, monsters, etc.

Combine the clay with the pipe cleaners and beads to create play meals, animals, bugs, objects, people, monsters, airplanes, cars, etc.! *(Examples are provided on the next page.)*

"Table-Top Letters"

Have your child make letters using items from your purse, luggage or *Activity Kit,* such as crayons, pencils, pipe cleaners, clay, etc. Challenge him by asking what letter he can make with just two crayons, then three, etc. Ask him to make another letter by taking away or adding one crayon (make a "W" turn into an "N" by removing the left side.) Next add some pipe cleaners and other items and make the rest of the alphabet!

"Clay Play" Examples

Fun Figures!

Use a pipe cleaner end to carve in details such as eyes, scales and a belly button for this mermaid (left). Use pipe cleaners to make spokes for wheels (car below.) If you embed a bead into each tire and place the pipecleaner through the beads, the car will roll!

Beads on pipe cleaners also create colorful legs that BEND, such as on this bird. Also, use the beads to add eyes and noses to create more elaborate designs.

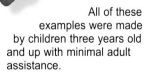

All of these examples were made by children three years old and up with minimal adult assistance.

Chapter 6

DOODLE PAD FUN

"Alphabet-Scribble Art"

Start with a letter, number or squiggle line on the *Doodle Pad,* note pad or other piece of paper. Have your child make a picture out of it (e.g. an "F" becomes a flag; an "M" becomes a mountain, etc.) An alternate game is to draw a line or curve and have your child make a letter or number out of it.

"Swinging Man"

A kid's variation of *Hang Man*. Draw him on a swing instead of hanging him. Leave blanks for a three-to-five letter word, and specify a category. Give hints if necessary. For each correct letter guessed, write the letter in the corresponding space. For each incorrect guess, draw a part of the man on the swing. Whoever finishes first, either by guessing the word or finishing the man, wins.

"What Am I Drawing?"

With a certain object in mind, the artist names a category. He begins to draw something within the named category (e.g. animal, food, object), then stops and asks, *"What am I drawing?"* The other players take a guess. The artist draws a little more and asks again, etc. The player must guess what is being drawn in five tries or less to win.

"Crowd-Pleaser Art"

The first artist begins by starting to draw an object. She then passes it around the table, asking everyone else to add something to the drawing. When it comes back around to the original artist, she should reveal what has been created!

As an alternative game, draw a family scene with a yard, trees, pets, etc. Pass it around for each player to add something to the scene. If there are only the two of you, pass it back and forth until you are satisfied with your picture.

Chapter 7

PREPARE to Scout

The following chapter contains a few scout tips that can be useful when traveling to strange places. You will learn about the five deadliest spiders and snakes, as well as how to tie several different types of knots. The images can be scary; teach your children using your discretion.

"Red & Yellow Can Kill A Fellow"

S nakes can be scary... if you don't know which ones can hurt you and which are harmless! The following descriptions and pictures can help you in your travels to become familiar with which species you should avoid if you happen across them while on a hike. It is important to identify the kind of snake you encounter in the unlikely event of a bite, so that the correct anti-venom can be given. The snakes described below are the five most venomous snakes found in the United States.

The Coral Snake: This colorful snake is commonly found in the south. Prefers moist areas near ponds or streams in hardwood forests, flat pine woods, rocky canyons and hills. Note that the red and yellow bands are right next to each other. To tell the difference between harmless snakes with similar colors and this one, remember: "Red and black is a friend of Jack; red and yellow can kill a fellow."

The Rattlesnake: Found all over the US, living in trees while, others, like the diamondback, live in the desert, as well as rocky terrain, canyons and marshes. Rattlesnakes are the most common venomous snake to cross our paths while hiking. They come in different sizes and shapes, but they all have one thing in common: the rattle. They will warn you if they see you first, but you must watch your step! If they have just eaten, they are commonly found sleeping in the sun stretched across your hiking path. Be careful not to step on it!

The Copperhead: This type of snake is commonly found in the southeastern US. It prefers living above streams or ponds in the wooded hillsides below, or at the edge of a swamp.

The Sidewinder: This species prefers hot, dry desert flatland with sandy washes or warm sand hammocks. It gets its name by the way it travels: "side winding" over surfaces, leaving a trail of parallel S-shaped footprints behind. They are nocturnal, and are usually sighted between sundown and midnight in spring. During the day, they live in mammal burrows or hide under the brush.

The Cottonmouth: These snakes are usually found in most parts of the SE U.S. and Missouri to south-central Oklahoma and Texas. They are very dangerous and aggressive in nature. They like to live in swamps, lakes, rivers, bay heads, sloughs, irrigation ditches and small clear rocky streams.

"Along Came a Spider..."

Spiders are another common, unwelcome guest in hotels, condos, rental homes and even airplanes! Listed below are the ones to avoid. Most of the others are harmless, although the sight of them may still give you the creeps!

The Black Widow: Black widows like to live anywhere in the US where it is warm, dark and has plenty of food. The warmer climates enable them to both breed and feed outside. The female carries the striking red marking on its underside, which can be an hourglass or dot shape. In general, any shiny black spider with a big, round abdomen should be avoided. The males are smaller, shyer, and may not even be poisonous! They look nothing like the females as they are usually thin and a mottled brown or gray color.

The Brown Recluse: These spiders wear the famous "violin shape" (see picture). It is one of the only spiders that has only six eyes! Most spiders have eight. In addition, their abdomen has no markings, and their legs are smooth with no thick hairs. Brown recluses have a smaller range than most people think, not straying further west than the Rocky Mountains and rarely venturing north of Nebraska. They prefer quiet, dark and warm places to raise their families, and don't travel as often with people like the black widow tends to do.

The Hobo: The hobo spider is the true culprit for countless numbers of spider bites blamed on the brown recluse. Both species look similar at a glance and their bite patterns and symptoms are almost identical. But hobo spiders have a more mottled color and distinctive 'herringbone' patterns on their abdomen, unlike the brown recluse, which has no markings there. The hobo's legs are also hairier. They are found throughout the Northwestern United States and Western Canada, areas in which the brown recluses do not live.

The Brazilian Wanderer: The Brazilian wanderer is the most toxic spider in the entire world. Not to worry, though, as *they are not found in the US*. These spiders are deadly and aggressive, attacking anything and anyone they see as a threat. They wander around, making them very hard to avoid. They're responsible for more cases of venom poisoning in Brazil than any other animal. The only good news is that only about a third of its victims are actually injected with venom. One can only survive this bite and live if the antidote is immediately available.

The Sydney Funnel Web: The runner up to the Brazilian wanderer is the funnel web spider of Australia. It is extremely dangerous, but it lives *only in Australia.* They are mostly terrestrial spiders, building typical silk-lined tubular burrow retreats. They live mainly in Sydney. Chances of being bitten are high if encountered, and the bite is lethal within 40 minutes if not treated.

"Knot So Boring"

Tying knots can be fun and can also come in handy when you need them! Here are a few popular types of knots found in the ***Boy Scout Manual***, along with a description of their most common uses. Use the jewelry string from your ***Activity Kit*** to practice them on the plane and see how fast you can master the art.

The Square Knot: This knot is probably the best known and most widely used knot. It serves to join the ends of two ropes, and is both strong and easy to tie and untie. People use square knots on packages and to fasten towing lines. It is also commonly known as the "first-aid knot."

1. Cross the two ends over each other, up and around through the loop to form a simple knot.

2. Bring the two ends up, giving yourself enough string to tie another knot.

3. Cross the ends over each other once again, and form a second knot above it.

4. Grab both ends and pull. The knot is secure and strong.

The Bowline Knot: One of the most-used loop knots, the bowline forms a strong loop that will not slip or jam at the end of a rope. A fun use of this knot is to have a friendly competition to see who can tie it around their waist the fastest.

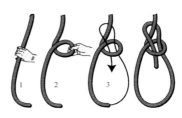

1. Grasp the string in the middle.

2. Make a loop in the center of the string.

3. Bring the end of the string up through the loop, around the other end and back down through the same loop as shown.

The Taught-Line Hitch: This is a remarkably useful knot; it's adjustable **and** trustworthy. It is the simplest of the adjustable knot family. Use a pencil with jewelry string provided in your *Activity Kit* to practice on the plane!

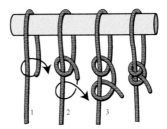

1. Wrap the string round the pencil and tie a regular knot, looping it around the string as shown.

2. Bring the string down and repeat step one, so that you have two loops around the string hanging down.

3. Pull on the end of the second loop until the knot is tight.

Chapter 8

MAGIC TRICKS

Items from your *Activity Kit* are needed for some of these tricks. Fascinate your children with these simple, clever tricks and let them have fun learning to perform them for you and their friends. *Tip: Make a magic wand out of pipe cleaners to add to the fun!*

"Disappearing Penny"

You will appear to make a penny vanish right before your child's eyes. Start by placing a penny in your open right hand, showing it to your audience. Next, pretend to grab the penny with your left hand, quickly dropping the penny into your lap with your right as you wave your left hand around as though it still has the penny.

Finally, rub both hands together and ask your child to say, "Abracadabra!" and show him both of your now empty hands! This trick can be performed with any small object, such as a small ball of clay.

"All Aces"

This trick will have your child holding all the aces from the deck magically in one pile after he watches you shuffle the cards over and over again.

First, find and place all four aces face-down in a row across the table. Deal out twelve more cards *going across* in rows until you have three additional rows of cards, for a total of four cards in each column.

Next, starting from the left, pick up each *vertical row*, keeping the aces at the top of each row, and gather them into a pile.

Shuffle the cards as many times as it takes to convince your child the aces are thoroughly mixed up. Next, lay the cards down in the same fashion, going across in rows, until you have four columns again. One of these columns will always have all four aces.

Ask your child to pick one of the four columns. If he happens to pick the column with all the aces on the first try, double magic has occurred! If not, let him keep guessing until he finds them. After all that shuffling, he will be amazed that they all wound up in the same pile.

"Pick A Card... Any Card!"

Y ou will be able to find your child's card no matter what card she picks and guess it right every time!

Let your child shuffle the deck as many times as she likes or do it yourself until she is satisfied they are completely mixed up. Once they are thoroughly shuffled, take the deck and find a way to glance at the bottom card and memorize it without being caught.

Next, have your child pick any card she wants while your eyes are closed. Tell her to look at it; remember what it is and don't tell you. Then have her place her card on the top of the deck.

Have her cut the deck and place the bottom part of the deck *on top* of her card, so that the card you memorized is not on top of her card. Spread the cards out face-up. Her card will be the one to the right of the bottom card you memorized. For added fun, tell her to concentrate on what her card is without telling you and to hold your forearm as you point. Go back and forth and then suddenly stop at her card and point to it, asking if you got it right!

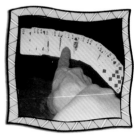

"The Great Napkin Break-Through"

This is a great magic trick finale! All you need is a paper napkin. The small, white cocktail napkins work best. Simply ask your flight attendant for a couple of them once you are comfortably seated on the plane.

Open it up fully into a big square and then start waving it around, covering your face and then suddenly popping out from behind it. My daughter and I do this while I sing "Da-da da-da, da-da da da-da," to the tune of the old song, *"Fine and Dandy."*

Finally, cover your face, pushing the napkin tightly over your mouth. Wait a second or two and then stick your tongue through it! (For an even bigger laugh, wiggle your tongue around!)

Children never seem to tire of this trick, no matter how many times they see it. All of the children I have done this trick for insist on performing it themselves and it is one trick that is completely safe, fun and easy for them to do.

Chapter 9

JUST WONDERING...

Back to more fun with the family and getting to know each other. These activities are fun and stimulating for all ages. We call them *Napkin Questions* simply because they are great for dinner table discussion.

"Playing Favorites"

Get to know your child. Add some of these answers to the *Memory Game* and later ask what someone's favorites (and least favorites) are.

- Number
- Color
- Food
- Pizza topping
- Place to visit
- Relative
- Way to travel
- Drink
- Season of the year
- Animal
- Dessert
- Cartoon character

- *Disney* movie
- *Disney* princess
- Superhero
- Time of day
- Bedtime story
- Part of bedtime routine
- Day of the week
- Month of the year
- Chore
- Outdoor activity
- Indoor activity
- Song

- Thing done at school
- Bike, trike, or scooter
- Hairstyle
- Room in the house
- Book
- Friend
- Piece of jewelry
- Type of car or truck
- Pet
- Art tool (paint, crayon)
- Flower
- Flavor of ice cream

"Would You Rather...?"

This game is little more sophisticated. Give two or more choices and have the player pick which situation he would rather have. Make them travel related. Ask the question, "Would you rather...? Why?" Here are a few to get started:

- Go to Mexico or Alaska.

- Ride on a plane, train or automobile.

- Fly really high or run really fast.

- Go to the mountains or to the beach.

- Visit _____ or _____ (name two very different people you need to take a plane in order to see.)

- Eat plane food or airport food.

- Have popping ears or jet lag.

- Be the Captain or a flight attendant.

- Sit on the aisle or near the window.

- Chew gum or drink water to prevent your ears from popping.

- Have some turbulence during the flight or a bumpy landing.

- Sit in the front, middle or back of the plane.

- Tell a joke or hear a story.

- Play Old Maid or Crazy Eights.

- Ride on a swing or go down a slide.

- Be short or fat.

- Drink from a cup or through a straw.

- Jump high or run fast.

- Play in snow or sand.

- Swim in the ocean or a lake.

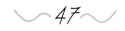

"What Would You Do...?"

These questions are a bit more philosophical and can help you teach values to your children. You can also find out what they think is right and guide them to the values you support. Ask the question, "What would you do if...?"

- You wandered away from the gate while waiting for the plane and got lost.

- A man you do not know at the airport offers you some candy.

- A flight attendant asks you to fasten your seat belt and put your tray table up.

- You have to use the rest room but you are sitting in the window seat.

- You are taking off or landing and your ears begin to hurt.

- You are bored on the plane and want to get up and walk around.

- The plane has landed and everyone is getting off the plane. You can't wait to get off, too, but your luggage is still packed up in the overhead.

- The captain turns on the seat-belt sign because of turbulence.

- You flew from a warm place to a very cold place and are about to go outside.

- The plane is going to land in a few minutes. You brought several toys with you, a few of which are on the seat and floor of the plane.

- You leave your favorite stuffed animal on the airplane and are already in the airport.

- As you are walking off the plane, you notice someone left a toy behind.

- A nice looking-lady at the hotel asks you to come to her car or room to see her new puppy.

"Straight Talk"

Here are some questions to get to know your family. Have fun and use your imagination. You will quickly come up with dozens of interesting topics and questions. Always ask, "Why?" Here are a few to get started:

1. What part of this trip are you looking forward to the most?

2. Who are you most excited about seeing?

3. If you had wings and could fly anywhere in the world, where would you go first?

4. This is your Magic Napkin. If it could grant you three wishes, what would you wish for?

5. What is the first thing you want to do when you get to your destination?

6. Tell us something new you did or learned about today.

7. Name three foods you are looking forward to eating on this trip.

8. Name your most and least favorite thing about flying on this airplane today.

9. Can you remember anything funny about a flight attendant or passenger?

Chapter 10

JOKES FOR KiDS

Travel "Knock-Knock" Jokes

Knock Knock.
Who's There?
Pakistan.
Pakistan who?
Pakistanwich. You
might get hungry!

Knock Knock.
Who's there?
India.
India who?
India-vent you don't
pack a sandwich, we
can get a hamburger.

Knock Knock.
Who's there?
China.
China who?
China to talk too loud!
I'm taking a nap.

Knock Knock.
Who's there?
Hawaii.
Hawaii who?
Hawaii doing on this
airplane trip?

Knock Knock.
Who's there?
Wayne.
Wayne who?
Wayne, Wayne go
away!

Knock Knock.
Who's there?
A European.
A European who?
Uh, You're a peein'
on my lawn! Use the
bathroom!

Knock Knock
Who's there?
Canada.
Canada who?
Canada Dry ginger
ale, please!

Knock Knock.
Who's there?
Kenya.
Kenya who?
Kenya please stop
kicking my seat??

Knock, Knock.
Who's there?
Minneapolis.
Minneapolis, who?
Even a mini apple is
enough to keep the
doctor away!

Knock Knock.
Who's there?
Oman.
Oman who?
Oh, man! Did you see that cool cloud?

Knock Knock.
Who's there?
Syria.
Syria who?
Seriously... check out that cloud!

Knock Knock.
Who's there?
Iran.
Iran who?
Iran so fast I beat the airplane!

Knock Knock.
Who's there?
Iraq.
Iraq who?
Iraq the boat, Uganda go splash!

Knock Knock.
Who's there?
Samoa.
Samoa who?
Samoa those crackers, please!

Knock Knock.
Who's there?
Ohio.
Ohio who?
When did you learn to yodel?

Knock Knock.
Who's there?
A cargo
A cargo who?
A car go beep, beep!

Knock Knock.
Who's there?
Carrie.
Carrie who?
Carry me! I'm too tired to walk!

Knock Knock.
Who's there?
Uganda.
Uganda who?
Uganda eat all that or can I have some?

Knock Knock.
Who's there?
Yellow.
Yellow who?
Yellow? Anybody home?

Knock Knock.
Who's there?
Idaho.
Idaho who?
Idaho where we're going, do you?

Knock Knock.
Who's there?
Dismay.
Dismay who?
Dismay be my very last Knock-Knock joke!

Silly Jokes

Q Miss Issippi (known as "Skippy"), asked Miss Ouri (in a hurry) what Virginia wore to the fair? But what, oh what, will Delaware??

A I don't know but, Alaska!

Q What does Tennessee?
A The same thing that Arkansas!

Q What is really big, is grey and has two trunks??
A An elephant on vacation!

Q What did the ocean say to the sun?
A Nothing. It just waved!

Q What did Tarzan say when he heard the elephants coming?
A "Here come the elephants!"

More Silly Jokes...

Q What do you get when you put three ducks in a box?
A A box of quackers.

Q What is an astronaut's favorite sandwich?
A Launch meat.

Q What does the mayonnaise say when you open the refrigerator?
A Close the door! I'm dressing!

Q If April showers bring May flowers, what do May flowers bring?
A Pilgrims!

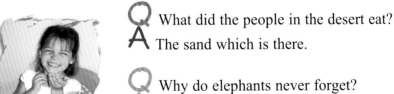

Q What did the people in the desert eat?
A The sand which is there.

Q Why do elephants never forget?
A Because nobody tells them anything!

Still More Silly Jokes...

Q What do you call a fairy that will not take a bath?
A Stinkerbell!

Q What kind of stories do ship captains tell?
A Ferry tales!

Q Where does a king keep his armies?
A Up his sleevies!

Q What is the biggest pencil in the whole world?
A Pennsylvania!

Q The terrible turtle took two chocolates to Texas to teach Thomas to tie his boots. How many "T's" in that?
A There are two T's in "THAT."

Q What exactly DID Delaware?
A Her New Jersey, of course!

The Last of the Silly Jokes!

Q Did you hear about the cab driver who lost his job?
A He drove all his customers away!

Q What did Cinderella say when her photos did not come in the mail?
A "Someday my prints will come!"

Q What goes up and down but does not move?
A Stairs.

Q What did the porcupine say to the cactus?
A "Is that you, Mommy?"

Q What has four wheels and flies?
A A garbage truck!

Q What is no bigger than a cup but not even a river can fill it up?
A A strainer.

APPENDIX A
"I Can, Can You?"

- Hold my fork and eat with my left hand. Now right hand.

- Draw a cat, smiley face, etc.

- Say the alphabet backwards and forwards.

- Count backwards from ten.

- Count to twenty / one hundred.

- Wink with one eye.

- Not kick the seat in front of me.

- Roll my tongue.

- Do the *Vulcan* greeting.

- Make this face.

- Make this letter with my hands.

- Sound like a cat, bird, etc.

- Rub my head and pat my tummy at the same time.

- Not whine the whole plane trip.

- Try something new to eat.

- State our flight number and mobile phone number.

- Chew with my mouth closed.

- Not interrupt.

- Say "Please" and "Thank you."

- Put my airplane seat-belt on.

- Make a goldfish face (suck in cheeks and move lips).

- Make eyeglasses out of my hands and wear them on my face.

- Make this sound with my tongue or mouth, (e.g. clicking, whistling or popping your cheek.)

- Close my eyes and touch my nose.

- Find the nearest exit and bathroom.

- Be polite to co-travelers.

APPENDIX B
"What Am I?"

OBJECT

- Number
- Vehicle
- Clothing
- Toy
- Shape
- Something hard
- Something soft
- Clock
- Phone
- Pen
- Water
- Sun

ANIMAL

- Farm
- Jungle
- Pet
- Ocean
- Land
- Soft

- Slimy
- Rough skin
- Slow or fast
- Dangerous
- Gentle
- Tall or short
- Skinny or fat
- Stings
- Bites
- Claws
- Horns
- Slithers
- Gallops
- Crawls
- Climbs
- Jumps
- Can fly
- Roars
- Squeaks
- Clucks
- Meows
- Barks
- Eats _____
- Is a color
- Has fur

FOOD

- Fruit
- Vegetable
- Snack
- Healthy
- Unhealthy
- Sweet
- Sour
- Salty
- Crunchy
- Hot
- Cold
- Meat
- Dairy
- Color

CHARACTERS

- Movie
- Cartoon
- Princess
- Superhero
- Biblical
- Historical

PLACE

- Where we've been
- Dangerous
- Safe
- Warm
- Cold
- Fun
- Near or far

PEOPLE

- Relative
- Public service
- Famous

ACTIVITY

- Outdoor
- Indoor
- Sport
- Team
- Individual
- Fun

APPENDIX C
"The Big Face-Off"

- Splashed with muddy water
- Stung by a bee
- Kissed by a bunny
- Licked by a puppy
- Stepped on hot sand
- Ice cream fell off cone
- Heard a really funny joke
- Lost favorite stuffed animal
- Shocked by static electricity
- Hugged by Mommy
- Tickled by a flower
- Tasted something sweet
- Tasted something sour
- Felt really full
- Startled by a loud noise
- Twirled until you were dizzy

- Asked a difficult question requiring much thought
- Spilled your water all over you
- Sat on ice cubes
- Smelled something really bad
- Smelled cupcakes baking
- Woke up at night by bright light
- Heard big monster steps
- Were just given tickets to Legoland, Disneyland, etc.
- Touched something really hot
- Rode on a roller coaster
- Pushed something really heavy
- Felt very, very sleepy
- Friend jumped out from behind a tree and startled you
- Fell off your chair

Name:

Flight Information:

Cell Phone:

Name:

Flight Information:

Cell Phone:

Name:

Flight Information:

Cell Phone:

Name:

Flight Information:

Cell Phone: